Oracle
of Destiny

9781646711345

U.S. GAMES SYSTEMS, INC.
179 Ludlow Street
Stamford, CT 06902 USA
www.usgamesinc.com

Editorial direction:
Balthazar Pagani

Graphic design
Davide Canesi / PEPE *nymi*

Editing
Caterina Grimaldi

Vivida

Originally Printed by Vivida

First Edition
10 9 8 7 6 5 4 3 2 1

Vivida® trademark is the property of White Star s.r.l.
www.vividabooks.com

© 2023 White Star s.r.l. | Piazzale Luigi Cadorna, 6 |
20123 Milano, Italia | www.whitestar.it

Translation: ICEIGeo, Milan (translation: Alexa Ahern;
layout: Chiara Giuliani)

All rights reserved. No part of this publication may be
reproduced, stored in a retrieval system, or transmitted in
any form or by any means, including electronic, mechanical,
photocopying, recording, or otherwise, without written
permission from the publisher.

Made in China

Oracle of Destiny

Written by
AZZURRA D'AGOSTINO

Illustrations by
PAOLA VECCHI

CONTENTS

• • •

Oracles of Destiny and Palmistry
p. 7

How to Read Hands: Some General Information
p. 12

How to Use This Deck
p. 17

Readings from the Deck
p. 18

The Cards
p. 25

Flexibility 26	Destiny 76
Humidity.................. 28	Destiny: Couple........... 78
Aridity....................... 30	Destiny: Absence....... 80
Hardness 32	Plain of Mars............ 82
Color.......................... 34	Ring of Solomon......... 84
Nails........................... 36	Monkey 86
Fire............................. 38	Intuition 88
Earth 40	Milky Way................... 90
Air............................... 42	Bracelet..................... 92
Water........................ 44	Sun.............................. 94
Roots......................... 46	Time............................ 96
Trunk......................... 48	Girdle of Venus 98
Branches................. 50	Influences................. 100
Mars.......................... 52	Affections................. 102
Jupiter...................... 54	Journeys 104
Saturn....................... 56	Concerns 106
Apollo........................ 58	Chains 108
Mercury.................... 60	Square....................... 110
Mount of Venus 62	Star............................. 112
Mount of Luna 64	Grille........................... 114
Life.............................. 66	Dot.............................. 116
Heart.......................... 68	Mystic Cross............... 118
Head: Rationality.... 70	Loop............................ 120
Head: Harmony 72	Arch............................ 122
Head: Dream............ 74	Whorl.......................... 124

Oracles of Destiny and Palmistry

Palmistry, or the art of palm reading, has been a widespread and well-established practice in many traditions since ancient times, from the East to the West.

We find hints of palmistry in some texts from Vedic India dating back to two millennia before Christ. China also has a written tradition of this art that predates the fourth century BCE.

In the West, there is a lack of sources from before the Middle Ages that refer to the subject, but there are traces of its widespread use among both the Greeks—in the texts of Aristotle, among others—and the Romans—like in the *Naturalis Historia* of Pliny the Elder.

The earliest known manuscript entirely devoted to palmistry in the English language dates to the 15th century: the *Digby Rolls 4*, a series of parchment strips sewn together to form a roll over two meters long.

Many works were produced between the 15th and 20th centuries, often connected to studies on astrology, alchemy, philosophy, and numerology.

Many thinkers and scientists in the past practiced palmistry, including Anaxagoras, Juvenal, and Paracelsus, but the list is so long and varied that it cannot be summarized in a few lines. Interest in palmistry, or chirosophy (defined as the art of seeing the character and psychological tendencies of an individual by interpreting his or her hand), probably derives from a fascinating principle: the idea that the body carries the signs of the soul reflected in stable details that can be cataloged and interpreted. The information they provide reveals the most intimate and profound aspects of a person, from their temperament to their inclinations and the way they relate to others. Sometimes they can also indicate their physiological characteristics or areas of greatest physical fragility. In certain cultures, such as Chinese, this idea is so well established that other parts of the body are also "read," including the feet and the face.

Although in ancient times palmistry was indeed one of the most common and practiced forms of divination, the information contained in this deck should not be taken as predictive or prophetic.

By delving deeper into the study of chiromancy, chirology (interpretation of hand lines), and chirognomy (interpretation of hand shapes), it becomes evident how the wisdom of these practices does not claim to develop a science of premonitions, but rather an alternative, creative, and transversal way of examining ourselves.

Hands are a privileged tool that we use to do work, explore, manipulate, and grasp the world. Extending the hand is the first gesture we offer when we meet someone.

The marks etched into this part of the body, along with the complex web of symbols and possible readings that have been applied to every detail over the centuries, open up an incredible and evocative world of possibilities for exploring our lives from a different perspective.

When we investigate ourselves, our actions, and our reactions with curiosity, often in order to go deeper and understand more fully and creatively the meaning and perspectives that arise in our experiences and relationships, we don't look only at the rational side.

Life is a tangle of emotions, ambitions, dreams, feelings, secrets, unconscious reasons, bodily impulses, and instincts. It's a difficult knot to untangle, but doing so helps direct our way of being and doing.

Thus, any tool that can stimulate our intuition and help us listen to ourselves and relate to things we can't understand with solely our intellect, can be a valuable ally in the great mystery of life.

The important thing is to be aware that there is no one method, no one way to deal with the challenges we face. Therefore, even the oldest disciplines and arts are not a means to be blindly relied upon for answers, but rather a trigger that can pique our curiosity and broaden the perspective we use to look at things.

We can read on the hand everything that is in us, depends on us, and dominates our relationship with the outside world. What about the future? If by "future" we mean knowing whether, for example, we will win some money, your hand won't give you an answer. But if we mean instead how much the future holds in our relationship with ourselves and with the outside world and how we will experience this relationship, which to a great extent is determined by our character, the state of health we are in, and our temperament, all these things are in some way written on the hand, and we can also modify them.

It is important to emphasize that the hand changes. The lines sometimes appear more prominent, sometimes more subtle; some details disappear, others stand out. It is our destiny that changes, guided by will, new awareness, and our actions.

This is how the cards of this guidebook came to be. It is not a simple compendium of information on chiromancy; but rather a series of suggestions drawing on this art form. It also physically involves the person using the deck, who is invited to search his or her hand for the proposed signs. This allows each person to explore the profound entanglement of life, fate, time, and the possibility of change according to personal interpretation.

How to Read Hands: Some General Information

The hand is like a map of our inner world and our relationship to the outer world. In its simplest approach, it appears to be composed of four zones.

Let us imagine dividing the hand vertically, with a line that runs along the axis of the middle finger and divides the base of the palm in half. One half contains the thumb and index finger. This is the outer part of the hand, which is related to the extroverted side of a person, ambitions, willpower, and the ability to be dominant. The other half will contain the ring finger and pinky. This is the inner part; the inner world of emotions and energy directed to the depths of our soul. The middle finger, called the Saturn finger, is the bridge between the two worlds, where they meet or collide in a constant search for balance.

If we then draw an imaginary horizontal line under the plump parts at the base of each finger (which are called mounts), we divide the hand into two more parts. One contains the fingers and mounts, which are connected to an individual's activity and his or her purely human intelligence. The other contains the rest of the palm and is inherent in the more passive (i.e., primordial, not strictly related to will) aspects of each person, along with those characteristics, such as instinct, that we have in common with other animals.

This division between external and internal worlds and active and passive lives already gives us important insights into what our hands can say about us and, our lives and the way we relate to the outside world.

Everything about the hand is examined: shape, color, skin texture, temperature, nails, flexibility, finger features, palm lines, fingerprints, moles, scars, tattoos, and rings.

Which hand do we read? There are many schools of thought regarding which hand should be prioritized. Some believe that more attention should be paid to the dominant hand (the one you write with), which would represent the current state of things and inherent possibilities. On the other hand, some say that the non-dominant hand (e.g., the left hand for non-left-handed people) should be read because it is less weary from daily use. Some choose which hand should be read according to gender. Others believe that the right hand represents the present and future development, and the left the past or gifts of birth. Regardless of the various points of view, it should be pointed out that both hands are always read so that one can compare the differences (they are never identical) and find similarities and patterns.

Each card in the deck represents a prominent feature in palm reading, and the meanings of each are briefly presented in this guidebook. The order of the cards in the guidebook reflects a possible general reading, ranging from the more outer and visible elements (texture to touch, shape, nails, fingers) to the more inner and articulated features (palm lines, finger-prints), just like a map, ranging from general morphology (borders, mountains) to increasingly detailed maps of cities (streets, squares).

Reading the guidebook independently of the deck gives you all the information you need to learn the basics of palmistry.

We can search our hands for the markings indicated on the cards and study their specifics, knowing that each element that emphasizes a part (moles, rings, tattoos) enhances and amplifies the overall meaning. Anything undersized (short, thin lines; short fingers; flat fleshy parts) usually indicates that we should pay attention to a possible deficiency in the properties of that element. The opposite (oversized, deep grooves; prominent features) denotes the presence of large, sometimes excessive qualities that might need to be moderated.

You will notice in looking for the marks on the hand that sometimes the lines are unclear, intertwined, or overlapping. You might even question whether it is the line you are looking for. This is normal; but with practice, like reading the hands of family and friends, recognizing lines and the possibilities they signify gets easier and easier. In addition, palmistry is an art of identifying relationships. Truth is not monolithic and absolute, but manifests itself both in the eyes of the beholder and in the relationship the fortune teller establishes with the person he or she is reading at that moment (even himself or herself). Follow your intuition. The line will appear and be the one you need for that circumstance.

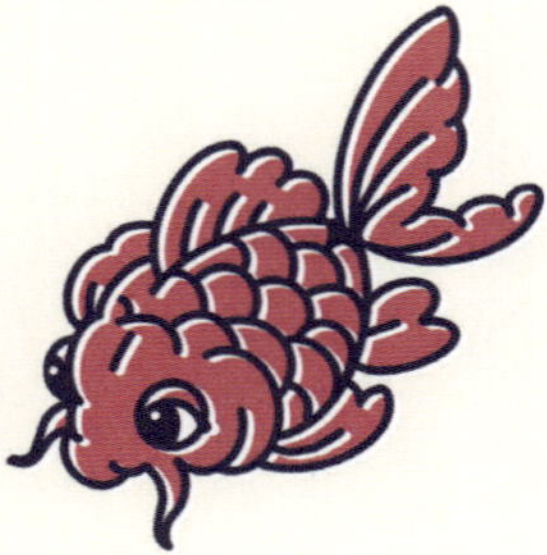

How to Use This Deck

The Oracle of Destiny contains fifty cards. The subject of each card is inspired by a characteristic of the hand and visually carries hints to the deeper meaning of that element. Exploring the image in detail offers an immediate emotional response, which awakens other channels beyond the conscious one.

It is advisable to consult the deck with pen and paper at hand. Each time a card is drawn, after careful observation of all the details, write down what the image evokes. It can be a list of words, a poem, a question, or a brief thought.

In this guidebook, the general meaning of each card is presented, as is the aspect of the hand and the divinatory meaning.

The explanation of the cards also includes a hand icon on which the areas the card refers to are highlighted in yellow. Use them to search your hand or the one you are reading.

Readings from the Deck

Three possible uses of the deck are described below, but everyone is free to invent their own.

The first type of reading, called the "Inspirational Card," can be used to investigate a concrete issue, a dilemma that is blocking our ability to act, leading us into an endless cycle of brooding that does not allow us to make a real choice. One way of intervening to break this cycle, which offers no solutions, may be to rely on our imaginative and metaphorical ability to introduce a completely different visual element, with its symbols and meanings, to activate a different way of thinking about that problem. The "inspirations" suggested on the card can thus elicit new questions, bringing about different and unexpected answers.

The second way to use the deck, is "Card of the Day," a practice used to pay attention to and be mindful of ourselves. I recommend keeping a journal with your cards in which you jot down everything relevant that happens to your spirit, body, and mind during the reading. It is important to make this time of day special and cherished by creating a small ritual that emphasizes the gift we are giving ourselves: paying attention to yourself from a perspective that is not just a performance. In this writing and reading session, we do not have to prove anything; we do not have to be efficient, good, or punctual. We just need to give ourselves some quality time. Let's lock ourselves in a room, knowing that we will not be interrupted. Let's make ourselves something to drink that we like and that feels good. Let's light a small, scented candle or some incense. Let's open a window to ourselves.

"Yesterday, Today, Tomorrow" is a three-card spread, useful when we feel we are at a turning point or desire a change. It may be a change imposed by a life cycle, such as choosing to undertake new studies or end a relationship. Or perhaps there is not a specific request that relates to the outside world. We do not have to choose a new job, but we may feel a pressing desire in ourselves, an inexplicable need to change something profound. This reading, both of the cards and the hand, will give us inspirations for how we are experiencing this urge, how we might deal with it, what we should pay attention to, what strikes us, and what sides of us will help us to develop this transition best.

Let's look at the three types of readings in further detail.

Inspirational Card

A problem is distressing you, an aspect of yourself is bothering you, a feeling of indecision is nagging at you. Try to find another way of looking at things, which may give you ideas you hadn't thought of.

While focusing on the issue at hand, draw a card from the face-down deck. Observe it and write down everything it brings to mind: the images, emotions, and thoughts it arouses. Think about what surfaces from the question you started with and try to figure out what message emerges from your subconscious through the words you wrote down and the feelings you felt. Consult the guidebook and read the meaning of the card, trying to find connections with your first inspiration. Check your hand for the features on the card you drew and see what the predominant element is. It will indicate both your predisposition to that element and the risks you might take if it is out of balance.

Card of the Day

If you want to explore what guiding element to follow, or what aspect to pay attention to on a certain day, draw a card from the face-down deck, observe it, and write down the words that the picture suggests. Then check the meaning of the card and go look in detail at what that mark looks like on the hand you are reading. It is the element that is puzzling you today, which should be humored or opposed, depending on the characteristics of the hand. Remember that any excessiveness (a particularly pronounced mark or its absence) indicates an imbalance that should be addressed.

Yesterday, Today, Tomorrow

Draw three cards and arrange them horizontally face down in front of you. Turn them over. The first will represent a general characteristic that has dominated your actions up to this point. The second indicates what drives you today. The third is what potential you have to deal with tomorrow. You can choose to write words for each individual card or for all three together. What question do they ask you, what challenge do they pose, and what possibilities do they open up for you? Consult the guidebook to read the meaning of each card, then check your hand to see what your physical characteristics say about it.

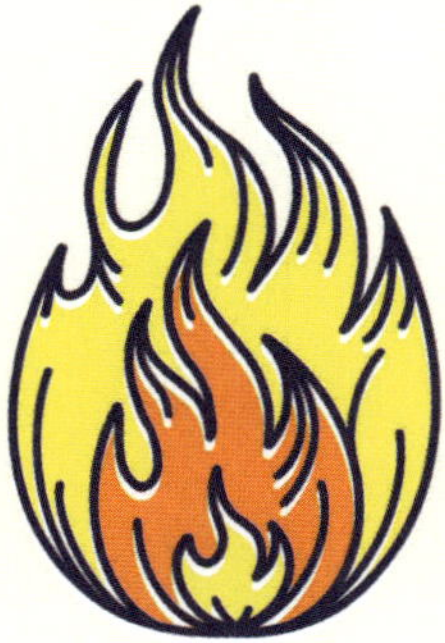

THE CARDS

Flexibility

ASPECT OF THE HAND

Flexibility, the fingers' ability to flex backwards, corresponds generally to how open one is. Checking the flexibility of a hand also means to probe the mind. It is a characteristic that changes over time, sometimes in surprising ways. The dominant hand shows the current state of the person, the non-dominant one the point from which one started as a natural inclination. Just as muscles can be trained by stretching, our mental openness can be expanded throughout life.

DIVINATORY MEANING

Don't shy away from new ideas. Don't be afraid of adventure. Of course we are alarmed by the unknown, because it asks us to question our sense of certainty. Live this openness as a gift without letting it overwhelm you. Being curious does not mean you don't have your own point of view.

Humidity

ASPECT OF THE HAND

If we imagine our hand as the surface of a living world full of underground rivers, the presence or absence of moisture on the palm is indicative of that invisible place. The rivers that flow within us are streams of emotions. When they surface up to our physically perceptible body part they can tell us more about our emotional level. Sometimes they reveal simple anxiety (like when we have sweaty palms before an exam). Other times they tell us that we are not managing our emotional side as we would like to, or as we imagine it to be socially acceptable.

DIVINATORY MEANING

Are you afraid to show how you truly feel? Of being judged, as not appropriate for a situation? Imagine that your job is to carry a lit candle from the other side of a lake. That lamp is your emotions. Protect the candle: don't let it fall into the water.

Aridity

ASPECT OF THE HAND

Even delicate and soft skin, which is indicative of sensitivity and natural refinement, can be parched. If moisture represents difficulty in handling the rivers of emotions, dryness connotes that they are restrained; that there is an inability to express yourself or even at times to understand what you feel. It is also a feeling of difficulty in letting go and truly believing what you feel. This characteristic can vary considerably throughout life.

DIVINATORY MEANING

Don't imprison what you hold most secret and dear. Imagine an ancient artist painting on the ceiling. Before finishing it, in the center he creates his most beautiful drawing. Then he covers it, so only God can see it. What do you think? Are you sure you don't want to show the rest of the world what you have to offer?

Hardness

ASPECT OF THE HAND

The skin is the largest organ and acts as a protective boundary of the body. It expresses our approach to the outside world. For that reason, rough, hard, and thick skin on the hands can correspond to metaphorically "having thick skin," or great physical resistance, but also can mean having strong emotional defenses. Of course, it depends also on the work we do, manual or otherwise, and this too will align with the way we perceive life and learn from experiences. This characteristic can vary considerably over time.

DIVINATORY MEANING

Life can hurt, it is true. It can be harsh, and you might feel the need to protect yourself. This is not a sufficient reason to harden your heart, bend to indifference, or demand too much of yourself.

Color

ASPECT OF THE HAND

In palm reading, "palm color" is a tint, and it depends on the flow and characteristics of the blood. It is as if we were looking at the color under the skin. It indicates how much vital energy the person has soaked up. There are variations. If one mount is more colorful than another, the characteristics of that mount are emphasized. If the color of the lines or nails does not match that of the palm (for example, if they have yellow, red, blue, or white shades) something is out of balance. It may be a sign of a physical issue, but also can indicate a defensive attitude toward life.

DIVINATORY MEANING

Each person has his or her own brightness, like a personal spectrum that does not depend on the color of the eyes, hair, or skin. There is a rainbow that emanates outward. We are the source of our light.

Nails

ASPECT OF THE HAND

Nails are a window to our health and temperament. Healthy nails are firm, compact and strong. The color is uniform, and the shape is in harmony with the rest of the hand. This is not always the case, and even the way we care for our nails speaks volumes. Long ones indicate sensitivity and low resistance. Short nails are a sign of an organized and methodical nature, which may tend toward anger. Square ones reveal a temperament that is lively and curious about everything; fanned-out suggests susceptibility.

DIVINATORY MEANING

With our nails, we scratch, but we also softly etch wax. Let's protect the most delicate part of our hands, which we bite when we are nervous. Let's play the harp and paint our nails. Nails teach us that everything depends on how you use what you have.

Fire

ASPECT OF THE HAND

A Fire hand, also called an intuitive hand, has an elongated palm and fingers that are not too long. Like in a bonfire, this type of hand emphasizes constant movement, the need to always be in action, as if to push away the intense emotional load that feeds every aspect of life, something that this type of person is particularly sensitive to. They also embody vivacity, the ability to convey enthusiasm, versatility, and the need to tame impatience and a short temper.

DIVINATORY MEANING

Fire burns; it is alive and full of energy. It penetrates things and warms them to the depths. If not controlled, it can be destructive. If it goes beyond the function of heating and cooking, of keeping things going and living, it can be lethal. Do not allow this to happen.

Earth

ASPECT OF THE HAND

An Earth hand, also called a practical hand, has a square palm and short fingers. It is characterized by being in close contact with the concrete elements of life and enjoying earthly aspects such as food, sex, and nature. The Earth is solid; it nourishes us; and although on the surface from a human perspective it appears motionless, under its thin crust it is alive and full of pressure. This kind of hand indicates that we have our feet on the ground. We can handle great physical exertion and embody honesty, dedication, and clarity of purpose.

DIVINATORY MEANING

The Earth is the force that sustains us, that can make trees grow. Let us allow ourselves to be guided by its natural rhythms and to instinctively understand the right time for everything. Let us move the body, let us listen to it. Let us enjoy life simply. The Earth is drying up. Can you hear the rivers flowing deep?

Air

ASPECT OF THE HAND

An Air hand, also called an intellectual hand, is characterized by a square palm and long fingers. Air transmits sound from one person to another; it is free, adaptable, moves with ease, and makes life on Earth possible. The Air hand tells us of the importance of communication, thinking, and making concrete and feasible plans. Originality, independence, care in relationships. Inner beauty and harmony. The predominance of thought over emotions.

DIVINATORY MEANING

Trust your inner self. Follow your enthusiasm for relationships with others. "Intellectual" comes from Latin and means the ability to feel, discern, understand, and see relationships between things. Show what you have that's valuable, without fear.

Water

ASPECT OF THE HAND

A Water hand, also called a sensitive hand, has elongated fingers and palm. It is very tapered and elongated in all parts. The superficial life often reflects that of the other side, and for this type of person it is less interesting than the deeper side, with which they are closely connected, giving the impression of being "dreamy." Introversion, intuition, secrecy, impressionability, moodiness, imagination, risk of losing touch with reality if one does not pay attention. They have many gifts, which could potentially overwhelm them.

DIVINATORY MEANING

Imagine that your inner world has the shape of a great goddess of the sea. She stays in the depths, in places that aren't visible, and rarely comes out. When she arrives, she is full of gifts: light, ancient animals, and clean water. But she is too big to be always with us, to find a home on the Earth. Can you be faithful to her without getting overwhelmed and sinking?

Roots

ASPECT OF THE HAND

The horizontal division of the hand allows us to identify three worlds: the one that occupies the most space on our hand tells us which type we belong to. If we imagine drawing the Tree of Life on our palm, the lower part of the tree, which runs from below the end of the thumb to the wrist, comprises the roots. This is the "physical world," the one dominated by passions and our relationship with earthly things.

DIVINATORY MEANING

At this time you are being asked to root yourself in the ground. To plant your roots into the moist matter of the world and nourish yourself on the pleasures and solidity that it can give you, without forgetting everything else. Or conversely, to pay attention to and control this tendency when it leads to neglect in the spiritual side of life.

Trunk

ASPECT OF THE HAND

Imagine a drawing of the Tree of Life on the palm, and then divide it horizontally to create three worlds: the largest one indicates which type we belong to. The part between the end of the thumb and the base of the fingers contains the trunk. This is called the "practical world." Here, we accomplish our tasks, achieve our aspirations, and can complete our work. Just as the trunk supports the tree, the practical world makes us effective.

DIVINATORY MEANING

No change is made without action. Improvement is not assumed: it is experienced. If you want to grow, like a tree that soars toward the sky from the Earth, you must work to strengthen your trunk and carry out your dreams.

Branches

ASPECT OF THE HAND

If we divide the hand horizontally into three "worlds," they each correspond to the three parts of the Tree of Life. The largest area indicates the type we belong to. The fingers are the branches of the tree. We call this part the "mental world," and this is where we plan, think, remember, create, and use logic and concentration. Just as the branches soar toward the sky, the head can be a valid guide that allows us to breathe.

DIVINATORY MEANING

Sometimes it is good to be an idealist, living in a world of thoughts and ideas. Don't lock yourself in an ivory tower; trust that you can reach upward through thinking, toward the light, like branches that reach for the sun.

Mars

ASPECT OF THE HAND

The thumb, also known as the finger of Venus and Mars, is central to palm reading because it presents, in a nutshell, all aspects of a person's nature. After all, it is the finger that allows us to touch what we come into contact with. The upper phalanx bone, the one with the fingernail, is related to willpower and determination. The one below it is related to logic and reason and indicates the degree to which they direct our intentions. When they are proportionate, we will succeed in carrying out intentions based on reasoning. The third phalanx is attached to the Mount of Venus, the seat of our vital energy.

DIVINATORY MEANING

This finger represents you in its entirety, capturing the essence of the way you master life by analyzing and reasoning before acting and doing. Venus, a window open to the ability to endure, love, rejoice, and experience pleasure. It is time to evaluate how you grasp what comes from the outside, and how you direct your rationality to achieve your goal.

Jupiter

ASPECT OF THE HAND

The index finger represents the attributes of the ancient king of the Roman gods: the ability to command and assert oneself and one's aspirations. It manifests the external world, the direction to take, and our adaptability to life. It does not necessarily mean to be successful, but rather to achieve the demands of our nature in life. If it is very long, it indicates an authoritarian attitude; very short, a lack of self-confidence. The characteristics related to it are ambition, leadership, honor, confidence, and a love of humanity.

DIVINATORY MEANING

It is not only the finger of leadership: it can also work magic, show you the way, or reprimand someone. It shows you are aware of your direction in the world, the need to listen to your abilities and aspirations and translate them into something concrete. Jupiter questions your decision-making power. Are you too strong willed? Do you impose yourself too little? Answer spontaneously to better address this aspect of your life today.

Saturn

ASPECT OF THE HAND

The middle finger takes on the characteristics of the planet and ancient god Saturn: an old hermit, reconciler of opposites, mediator between the urges of the inner and outer worlds. Saturn is the place where the two worlds meet, the magic finger of the axis of destiny, the point of balance between all the tendencies revealed by the other fingers. A wise old man, a philosopher, a scientist, a drawbridge.

DIVINATORY MEANING

Saturn is a solitary god because no one can learn our lesson for us. He teaches us discipline and autonomy. He leads us to transform the existing order to generate a new state of things. The appearance of Saturn is inviting you to thoroughly investigate and enforce your limits, the boundary beyond which you do not allow the outside world to suggest to you. Consider your relationship with the distances you have to set. You mustn't allow yourself to be invaded. Can you do this with the right balance, without going so far as to isolate yourself?

Apollo

ASPECT OF THE HAND

The ring finger is related to the qualities of the ancient sun god Apollo because of the properties it represents. It manifests a tendency to be sunny and optimistic, toward a love of beautiful things, art, and play. It also represents relationships with one's community, friends, and significant others. It is directly linked to the heart. Creativity, charisma, artistic ability lie here. Beware of your ego and narcissism.

DIVINATORY MEANING

Apollo was not only the god of the Sun but also of music, prophecy, the arts, and medicine. Have confidence in what cannot be seen. Follow the direction of your emotions and intuition, and trust in the good. You will be able to heal and make predictions. The creative capacity is always intuitive. Rely on it, but do not think about it too much when contemplating your image reflected in the mirror of time.

Mercury

ASPECT OF THE HAND

The pinky finger is that of intuition, dialectical, and commercial skills, but also of the relationship with one's family of origin, with the tight, carnal relationship with another, and finally with one's inner child. It is connected to the god Mercury, who appears frequently in mythological tales. Many of his attributes are recognizable in the personality of the archetypal Mercurian. He is famous for the wings of his sandals, which made him the messenger of the gods.

DIVINATORY MEANING

To the Greeks, Mercury was a teacher, a god, a king who could perform magic, transmit wisdom, and write. He brings the desire and ability to communicate with others on many levels. He guides our relationship with money, sex, and our ancestors. Not only that, but he is also the carrier of dreams that guards and transmits the messages of childhood that still exist in us. Now is the time to listen to your inner child. It will know how to guide you to places of inspiration, to the root of what you need.

Mount of Venus

ASPECT OF THE HAND

The Mount of Venus is the fleshy part of the palm that is located below the thumb. Venus, the goddess of both carnal and spiritual love, inspires the forces contained in this place, a taste for the pleasures of life, from good food to sex and beautiful things. Lover of the god Mars and mother of Cupid, Venus tells us of the energy that we have at our disposal, which we should draw on to cope with life. The Mount of Ven@@@s protects our stamina, which is our ability to access the most important reserves of vital energy that exist: love.

DIVINATORY MEANING

Here lies your deepest reserve of energy, your safe, your storehouse. Think of the thing that is most powerful to you: a hug, the sea, a memory. When you feel tired, when you need to regenerate, when you are in difficulty, go to your Mount of Venus. Therein lies your strength, in that place you have seen.

Mount of Luna

ASPECT OF THE HAND

The Mount of Luna, the fleshy part of the palm at the base of the pinky finger, represents our irrational part, that which lies beyond the conscious: intuition, imagination, dreams, sensitivity. It is the place where resources are hidden, which should be used to grasp the subtle elements of existence. If very flat and rigid, it reveals that one is afraid to delve into their dark side. When pronounced, the person is charismatic and in touch with deep feelings. A grille of lines on the Mount of Luna indicates melancholy.

DIVINATORY MEANING

Full of craters, bright and mysterious, this spot holds your most hidden side, the things you don't know about yourself, your creativity. It is a mountain you can only descend. There are doors to stairs and windows open to the dark. There are your secrets and the things you have yet to invent, the words you said as a child and have forgotten. Look inside and explore.

Life

ASPECT OF THE HAND

The Life Line generally starts between the thumb and index finger and surrounds the Mount of Venus (the fleshy part below the thumb). It does not indicate the duration of one's life, but the amount of vital energy. It draws its properties from the Mount of Venus, including endurance, health, and strength. When it is straight and clearly traced, it is like a groove in a plowed field: solid, ready to let our life sprout. If it is broken, this can indicate a great change: a relocation, a choice that turns everyday life upside down, a significant turning point.

DIVINATORY MEANING

Our life asks to be considered. It can tell us that we are living fully or spur us to consider our failures and fears. When it is broken, it teaches us about the strength hidden in the crisis. You have everything you need to live fully: energy, strength, and a capacity for transformation. Even the most painful changes can be an engine of growth if you know how to treasure them.

Heart

ASPECT OF THE HAND

The Heart Line starts on the side of the palm below the pinky finger, cuts across it, and ends generally between the index and middle finger. It tells us about our relationship with all events related to feelings, thus not only love relationships but also friendships, spiritual unions, and any aspect concerning our heart. It can be interrupted and start again at another point, which represents a broken heart, or the experience of deep pain or something that has hurt our feelings.

DIVINATORY MEANING

Our life asks to be considered. It can tell us that we are living fully or spur us to consider our failures and fears. When it is broken, it teaches us about the strength hidden in the crisis. You have everything you need to live fully: energy, strength, and a capacity for transformation. Even the most painful changes can be an engine of growth if you know how to treasure them.

Head: Rationality

ASPECT OF THE HAND

The Head Line starts at the palm, between the thumb and forefinger, and crosses the palm toward the Mount of Luna. When it is oriented toward the Mount part, perhaps with a well-marked, straight groove, it indicates a person guided by intellect. Rationality is its main resource; the ability to concentrate and logic are valuable traits to rely on. But they also can carry the risk of overlooking the signs of the unconscious and how much of the world cannot be explained by the mind alone.

DIVINATORY MEANING

The talent you need right now seems to be rationality, the ability to analyze and find logical solutions. Seeing laws where chance seems to reign, like Newton, who intuited universal gravitation from an apple falling from a tree.

Head: Harmony

ASPECT OF THE HAND

If the Head Line is oriented toward the middle of the Mount of Luna, this indicates well-developed reasoning, pliability, and great understanding, as well as imagination and a relationship with one's darker inner world. Those who have the line in this position do not lose contact with the unconscious, nor with logic or the talent of rationally analyzing situations.

DIVINATORY MEANING

Tap into Dorothy's confidence in the *Wizard of Oz*: she knows the safety of her home, but also allows it to fly away in a tornado. One of the greatest gifts is to create harmony between the rational and the irrational, to know how to grasp the infinite nuances that bind black and white.

Head: Dream

ASPECT OF THE HAND

When the Head Line ends under the Mount of Luna, it points to a container of secrets, the unconscious and the imagination. Rationality is subjugated by it. It's as if the invisible becomes more alive and concrete than the visible: as if contact with reality is lost.

DIVINATORY MEANING

There is great richness in turning away from the everyday, in blindly trusting one's intuitions, in experiencing one's visions as a real thing. Embrace these gifts, but be careful not to overdo them. The dream directs and plants clues, but it is not the only dimension of life. Nothing can feed us when there is too much of it.

Destiny

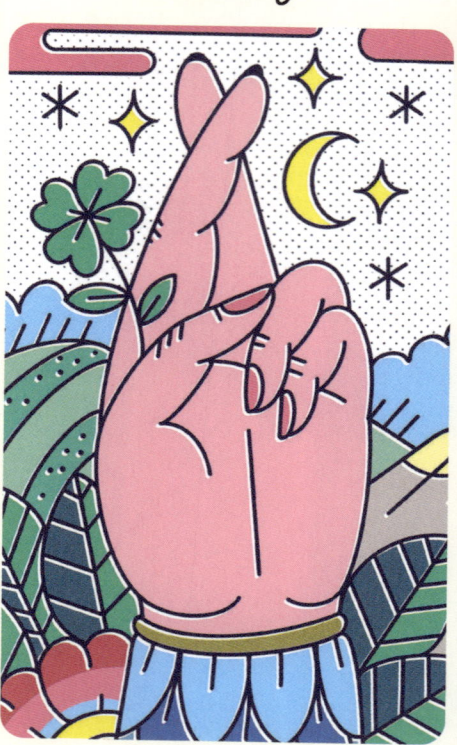

ASPECT OF THE HAND

The Line of Destiny starts at the wrist and runs vertically through the hand. It is also called the line of Saturn or Fortune. It represents the talents and gifts we had at birth, but also the risks we take according to our nature. It is about everything inevitable. It can be present on both hands, just one, or absent. When it is present only on the left hand, it indicates that to fully realize our destiny, we will have to return to our childhood dreams. If it is only on the right hand, we are contributing as adults, with our will, to achieve what we were born to do.

DIVINATORY MEANING

Not everything is written in stone, but from birth we have a set of characteristics that affect our lives. It is necessary to consider, enhance, or mitigate them according to a certain need. Fulfilling our destiny starts with us. Are you ready to become who you are?

Destiny: Couple

ASPECT OF THE HAND

The Line of Destiny crosses the palm vertically from the wrist. It concerns what is given, representing the talents we possess from birth and the risks associated with our temperament. When it is present on both hands, it indicates a great balance between past and future, between potential and implementation. We are fully realizing what we have received as a gift.

DIVINATORY MEANING

A tightrope walker challenges themself by walking on ropes over ravines, skyscrapers, high-rises, and rooftops. Likewise, you walk through life with the balancing pole in your hand balancing your desires and the fulfillment of your potential. Fear not, and you will not fall.

Destiny: Absence

ASPECT OF THE HAND

The Line of Destiny runs vertically up the palm from the wrist and represents all the gifts we received at birth and the risks that our temperament holds. When it is not visible on either hand, however, it does not mean that we do not possess distinctive characteristics or gifts at birth. Rather, it indicates a feeling of scorn toward conditioning and that we have total freedom in important life choices.

DIVINATORY MEANING

Sometimes we do not know as children what we want to be when we grow up. This can be frightening but also conveys a great sense of freedom. Allow yourself to experience everything. Be confident in experiencing new things in life. This is the best way to discover your true talent.

Plain of Mars

ASPECT OF THE HAND

This plain that opens in the center of the palm is also called the "bed of Venus and Mars" or "the ocean in one's destiny." It is a place of confrontation, a sign of the boldness to which we appeal in facing or undertaking the battles that we deem right or that become necessary in the course of our lives. The clearer and wider it is, the more it is a sign of generosity and balance.

DIVINATORY MEANING

The plain opens up, and we find ourselves there, perhaps equipped, well-trained; sometimes lost, troubled. But it will happen sooner or later, this is certain. It is a battle with an external or internal enemy, with instances of life or events that we have caused. What matters is having confidence in our courage, respect for what we are facing, and awareness that it is time to be open to confrontation.

Ring of Solomon

ASPECT OF THE HAND

This is a loop that the Heart Line forms by wrapping itself around the base of the index finger. It is the ring of magicians and Kabbalists, a sign of wisdom and spiritual and psychological abilities. It indicates an ability to intuitively read others, interest in metaphysical topics, and, as indicated by the name of the great biblical king, exceptional inner balance. It is an invitation to always be on the lookout, under the guidance of selflessness, listening, and idealism.

DIVINATORY MEANING

King Solomon received the gift of wisdom directly from God. For seven years he devoted himself to building an extraordinary temple full of gold, of which nothing remains but the memory. Similarly, his valuable but symbolic ring reminds you to trust intuition as an inner talent in handling human worries.

Monkey

ASPECT OF THE HAND

The Simian Line cuts across the hand horizontally, from below the little finger to the index finger, and manifests itself when the Heart and Head Line coincide. Its presence indicates that emotions take the upper hand, preventing rationality from taking over. Thinking, in this case, is feeling, and attention is focused on what stands before you from moment to moment. It can represent something brutal, in its tracing back everything to the senses by eliminating rationality. It complicates relationships with others. It is like a chaos of presences. One does not discern with the mind but with perception and emotions. In China and Japan, it is considered a sacred sign.

DIVINATORY MEANING

The statues of many Eastern enlightened people possess this line, which asks us not to forget our spiritual path and not to lose sight of our goals. In art, it involves compulsively living creativity. The card invites you not to forget the needs of others in order to become wholly fulfilled.

Intuition

ASPECT OF THE HAND

The Intuition Line is located below the little finger. As the name implies, it strengthens you with the power of intuition, imagination, and extrasensory perception. It enhances one's talent for understanding human nature and communication skills. Rising from the Mount of Luna, a place of imagination and the unconscious, it releases purely mental energy. It is the source from which many artists draw inspiration and requires delicacy. Perceiving beyond the visible can make one overly dreamy or nervous.

DIVINATORY MEANING

It is a time to close one's eyes, to open your view to something greater. There are forces in you that can pick up on the collective unconscious. Express your empathic nature, and fully trust your intuition. Do not make yourself available on command. This is the time to follow your personal rhythm.

Milky Way

ASPECT OF THE HAND

This is a rather rare line, sometimes composed of several parallel dashes that begin and end on the Mount of Luna. It is also called the Via Lascivia. It is a sign of great openness to the sensations of and relationship with our bodies. It represents great physical dynamism and a strong inclination to sensory pleasures; vitality and health emanate from this line. In extreme cases, it can indicate the feeling of being too sensitive for this world. In this case, it denotes a tendency toward mysticism and strong gifts for the occult.

DIVINATORY MEANING

Sometimes we become afraid of what we have inside: a tendency toward vices, for example, or the feeling of being hypersensitive toward an increasingly aggressive, polluted world. This fear should not be denied. We can embrace it and transform it, realizing that fragility is a strength, capable of showing us hidden aspects of reality.

Bracelet

ASPECT OF THE HAND

The Bracelet is a line drawn where the hand encounters the wrist. There can also be two or three lines. They represent health, luck, and happiness, three elements that are rather elusive and difficult to retain. For that reason, when all three are present together and well defined, they are also called the Regal Bracelet, indicating exceptional dynamism and protection toward success. When a cross is found there, one can hope that all their efforts will be richly rewarded. Each line of the bracelet is also called the Rascetta and can provide information about the organs of the abdomen.

DIVINATORY MEANING

It is time to trust in the circles of magical protection that can come to our rescue as a gift. Not everything depends on our will and action, but everything relates to the way we welcome what comes our way. On your wrist, a bracelet tinkles magically, invisible, carefully guarding the hidden parts of you.

Sun

ASPECT OF THE HAND

The Sun Line originates at the lower edge of the palm, not far from the Line of Destiny, and cuts it vertically, ending at the root of the ring finger. It is very rare and is also called the Line of Glory. Regardless of how straight or deep it is, it is a sign of a satisfactory professional life. If it is present only on the left hand, the generosity of heart will dominate aspirations. If only on the right, it is a favorable omen of conditions that come to the aid of our will.

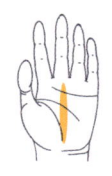

DIVINATORY MEANING

The Sun Line tells you to fully trust in your abilities, your merits, and your efforts, in order to realize and bring your aspirations to fruition. Everything you need does not depend on the outside, but is already present in your intuition, your dedication, and your talents. Give them space.

Time

...PECT OF THE HAND

Time is only seemingly fixed and determined. The one marked by clocks and calendars is measurable, but there is also a point-like one, connected to our experiences, which scans our lives in a personal way. To retrace time in years, you can draw a line on the palm from the middle finger that crosses the Life Line. This point corresponds to the first ten years of life. There are no rules for marking all the steps. What matters is becoming aware, even physically, of the flow of time.

DIVINATORY MEANING

Sometimes, the future is represented behind us. Only the present and the past are visible to us. More than birthdays, other events often count to mark a transition: a discovery, a love, a loss. Get in touch with your inner time and have no anxiety about having to conform to the stages planned by others.

Girdle of Venus

ASPECT OF THE HAND

This line begins between the index finger and the middle finger and can be considered subsidiary to the Heart Line. The fact that it is present indicates increased emotional sensitivity. It connects the physical world and the intimate world of the personality. It unites the elements of self-affirmation with emotions, and may for this reason indicate a continuous need for excitement and variety. If short, it is a sign of healthy emotional readiness; if fragmented, it may indicate very high and unstable sensitivity.

DIVINATORY MEANING

You can choose whether your sensitivity is a gift or a curse. Perhaps, sometimes both your senses and your emotions are more acute than those of others. This can help develop your creative powers. But if you allow yourself to become overwhelmed, you will be at the mercy of forces you feel you cannot control, with the risk of losing yourself.

Influences

ASPECT OF THE HAND

The Lines of Influence show the possibilities of love and union and are the only lines on the hand that represent the other people in our lives. They are vertical, mainly on the Mount of Venus, and run parallel to the Life Line. They are often thin and pale, and therefore not easy to detect. They provide clues to the possibility of relationships and our emotional receptivity. On the non-dominant hand, they show who influences our hearts; on the dominant hand, they show how others experience our influence.

DIVINATORY MEANING

Parents, siblings, mentors, close friends, and even enemies can manifest themselves in us. How much good we retain from the presence of each important figure in our lives depends also on how free we are from the influence of others. Everything affects us and changes us, but this is different from allowing ourselves to be subjugated.

Affections

ASPECT OF THE HAND

The Affection Lines are on the fleshy part below the little finger, called the Mount of Mercury, and they start from the outer part of the hand and run toward the center of the mount. They are short parallel lines and are purely indicative. On the dominant hand, they indicate the hearts you have touched. Whereas on the non-dominant hand they represent how many have touched your heart. A solitary line, or one longer than the others, indicates deep love, a lasting relationship.

DIVINATORY MEANING

There is a time when it becomes necessary to take care of one's relationships, of your closest loved ones, by hugging more often, listening and telling them that you love them. Nothing is taken for granted or given once and forever, especially in matters of the heart. Look inside yours, and you will know what you need to do.

Journeys

ASPECT OF THE HAND

Journey Lines are short lines that may begin at the bottom of the Mount of Luna or along the Life Line. They increase the influence of the Moon and the enjoyment of travel. They indicate that we do not like to stop for too long and that we are not afraid of change. Should external conditions not allow us to undertake physical journeys to discover the world, we must undertake inner journeys to not give up traveling. With the help of books, maps, computers, and especially the imagination, we can visit ever-changing scenes. The longer and more defined the signs, the farther and longer we will travel.

DIVINATORY MEANING

The answer right now is to change the landscape. Do it through an archaeological expedition, a fun outing, a spiritual pilgrimage, or a philosophy conference. The need is the same: to set out in search of discoveries.

Concerns

ASPECT OF THE HAND

This series of horizontal lines that run along the Mount of Venus represents challenges, downfalls, events, and problematic people that have intersected our lives. They can be all along the Mount; or a few, many, one or none. If none of these lines cuts across the Life Line, it indicates a problem that has not yet made itself manifest. If they are numerous, they tell us of a tumultuous existence, continually marked by minor discomforts but also of the need for life energy to be directed toward the outside world.

DIVINATORY MEANING

You are not your problems. You are not even your traumas. Try to take better care of your energy. It is not unlimited and there is no need to be hypervigilant all the time. Dedicate yourself to listening more deeply. Worries are not thoughts.

Chains

ASPECT OF THE HAND

Any line can look like chains, making it irregular and poorly defined, visually similar to a chain. In general, they indicate that aspect of life will not be experienced linearly: we will face indecisions, obstacles, setbacks, and struggles. On the Head Line, it means uncertain ideas and fickle memory. On the Heart Line, it is a warning that says to learn to follow your heart more.

DIVINATORY MEANING

Something binds us, preventing us from going more deeply and freely into what we are experiencing. Perhaps we are not following our hearts; maybe we are letting our minds get confused; maybe we make impulsive decisions that we regret. It is time to free yourself from your chains.

Square

ASPECT OF THE HAND

A square is a modifier sign, and its meaning depends on its position on the hand. In general, squares always represent an intervening protector against danger. Under Saturn, it will defend against accidents. On the Head Line, it will protect us from danger. On the Destiny Line, it will prevent incorrect financial action. On a Journey Line, it means we can depart without apprehension.

DIVINATORY MEANING

Can a geometric mark on the skin be your protector? Perhaps you are not different from your body, and you can trust that a powerful and beneficial element lies in you. Always and always, regardless of whether you make yourself visible or not. Appeal to the forces that animate and guide you, for this is a time to take chances.

Star

ASPECT OF THE HAND

If the palm is a sky, the Stars are what illuminates our destiny. They can appear in many places on the hand and bestow their benefits on the element where they are found. For example, on the Mount of Venus, they can indicate a stable and lasting union; on that of Jupiter, (under the index finger) they represent a complete worldly success; on that of the Luna, a formidable creative ability. It is the star of stars.

DIVINATORY MEANING

When a Star appears on our horizon, something that runs through the whole universe moves in us: desires, inspirations, deep communication with the cosmos, awe, a sense of beauty, of being part of something great. Each of us can be a star.

Grille

ASPECT OF THE HAND

Grilles, crisscrossing lines, can be found in various places on the palm and indicate an imbalance. They can partially or completely contradict the indications of the Mount on which they are found. They should be observed so that you don't make your success illusory. To confront them is to face difficulty. They can irritate, or act as a magnet. Irradiant, they demand attention. If they are on the Mount of Venus, they make the person attractive, though not always toward the right partner, with the possibility of suffering.

DIVINATORY MEANING

Difficulties and setbacks can sometimes teach us that true happiness is the happiness we share. From imbalances, we can learn new ways of being part of a relationship, sharing joy and learning—because courage is not the absence of fear or not being afraid to be wrong. It comes from the ability to take chances by facing adversity.

Dot

ASPECT OF THE HAND

Dots are also referred to as Spots. Often their presence is only temporary and indicates a sudden and solvable obstacle regarding the favorable indications provided by the Mount or Line on which they are located. Their disappearance coincides with the end of the difficult period. They can be white, black, dark blue, or red. On the Heart Line, they might indicate emotional suffering.

DIVINATORY MEANING

"We have reached the point," it is said when you strike the heart of the issue in a situation or relationship. We can take note that it has not been as simple as we thought, that we are facing difficulty. Thanks to this realization, we can face anything and we are already on the way to a solution.

Mystic Cross

ASPECT OF THE HAND

Crosses can appear all over the hand. They often cut across the lines or are found on a Mount. When they appear, one must pay particular attention to the characteristics of that element. Because crosses put people on alert, they signal that a problem may arise. One particular cross is the Mystic Cross, which has a different meaning. It stands between the Heart Line and the Head Line. To carry its full meaning, it must not touch them. It indicates a propensity for and skill in philosophy, theology, and occultism. It may be present from birth or appear at some point in life, perhaps after a strong spiritual experience.

DIVINATORY MEANING

The cross comes to the rescue, manifests as a calling, and represents the more subtle and spiritual aspects of existence. Trust it, don't fight it, and take in the deeper elements of life.

Loop

ASPECT OF THE HAND

The Loop is the type of fingerprint that is most commonly found. As the name indicates, it can be described as a line folded back on itself to form a kind of narrow noose. Sometimes, it is found on the finger of Apollo (ring finger), only very rarely on the finger of Saturn (middle). When it is present on all fingers, it signifies perceptiveness, a mild but strong-willed temperament and a tendency to be cold in judgment and harsh when dealing with business. It can also indicate an inclination for melancholy.

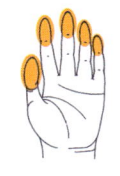

DIVINATORY MEANING

The noose can ensnare and draw in, like a thrown lasso. Trust in your more solid side, the one that tells you what is right and wrong, that makes you choose without too much doubt, that makes you immediately intuit what position is most consistent with your nature or the needs of that moment. Trust also in the fact that you can listen to your gentler, more somber side without ending up in a trap.

Arch

ASPECT OF THE HAND

This type of fingerprint has a simple shape but is not very frequent; it is generally found on the index finger. Since it is often on the finger of Jupiter, it indicates that one is eager to succeed, ambitious and convinced of their certainty to the point of being contentious, if not rebellious. On the positive side, this manifests as self-confidence; on the negative side, it can result in selfishness.

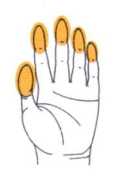

DIVINATORY MEANING

An arch connects one bank to the other. It is the shape of a rainbow with its magical fruits, and it can be a period of time that unites the past and future. Everything is held, even what seems far away.

Whorl

ASPECT OF THE HAND

This type of fingerprint develops its concentric pattern around an epicenter in the middle of the fingertip. It is the most complex feature and also indicates psychological variety. The general characteristics are being reserved, restlessness, sensitivity, and perceptiveness. A whorl on one finger is a sign of independence regarding the characteristics of that finger, of free interpretation of those values. On the ring finger, it indicates a desire for originality in expressing oneself.

DIVINATORY MEANING

You can find new means of personal and nonconformist expression. Propose original solutions in dealing with relationships, business, and every aspect of life. Trust in your originality, and never forget that you should not impulsively give in to an anxious need to act. Hesitation can be fruitful if accompanied by thought.

About the Creators

AZZURRA D'AGOSTINO

An author and chiromancy enthusiast, Azzurra was born and lives in a small town in the Tuscan-Emilian Apennines. She has published several collections of award-winning poetry, and she writes for both adult and children's theater, collaborating with dancers and visual artists. She has published children's books and a children's novel for DeA Planeta Libri. In addition to writing, she leads poetry workshops for people of all ages and is the founder of the SassiScritti Association.

PAOLA VECCHI

Paola is an Italian illustrator and graphic designer. She lived and worked in Spain for ten years until she moved back to Italy in 2019, to the shores of Lake Maggiore, where she continues her career path. She uses both digital and analog techniques and creates murals and pictorial works in addition to illustrations for publishing. Her style is made up of bold lines and colors. She is mainly inspired by her inner world, while often making references to pop culture.

Notes

For our complete line of tarot decks, books, meditation cards, oracle sets, and other inspirational products please visit our website:

www.usgamesinc.com

Follow us:

U.S. Games Systems, Inc.
179 Ludlow Street
Stamford, CT 06902 USA
203-353-8400
Order Desk 800-544-2637
FAX 203-353-8431